Conker Editions Ltd
22 Cosby Road
Littlethorpe
Leicester
LE19 2HF
Email: books@conkereditions.co.uk
Website: www.conkereditions.co.uk
First published by Conker Editions Ltd 2021.
Text © 2021 Mark McCarthy.

The publisher makes no representation, express or implied, with regard to the accuracy
of the information contained in this book and cannot accept any legal responsibility for
any errors or omissions that may be made.
A CIP catalogue record for this book is available from the British Library.
13-digit ISBN: 9781999900885.
Design and typesetting by Gary Silke.
Printed in the UK by Mixam.

101
MANCHESTER
CITY
MATCHWORN
SHIRTS

The Players - The Matches
The Stories Behind the Shirts

Mark McCarthy

CONKER

Contents

Introduction

A visit to my grandfather's house on a Sunday evening was something I always looked forward to as a child but one particular trip in December 1983 was to change the course of this nine-year-old's life forever. He would always have a story to tell but that day's tale was by far the best yet, as he informed me that my cousin would be joining Manchester City. I knew nothing about football at this stage, nor did I follow a team or even own a football shirt – but from that moment on, I was simply hooked.

As the years ticked by it was always my goal to own a shirt from Mick's time at City. That childhood dream became a reality when I finally sourced a shirt of his from a dealer who was selling up his City collection. It was only ever my intention to own just the one shirt... however, my collection now stands at 410 original matchworn or issued City shirts, dating back to the 1926 FA Cup final.

There was something about receiving Mick's shirt that day that kicked off my passion for collecting City match shirts: it was the smell and feel of the shirt coupled with the feeling of being lost in time, reminiscing about the dressing rooms the shirt had been in, the battles it had been involved in during the two seasons from 1985 to 1987. Of course, it's very different these days, with the players wearing so many shirts per season. I recall Mick telling me that the shirts were virtually counted on and off the players backs – and the great Mike Summerbee once told me that if shirts were torn back in the day, the players themselves would have to get them repaired before the next game. This was still the case in 1996 when Georgi Kinkladze's shirt was torn and simply sewn up for the next fixture.

As a collector, when you eventually track down a shirt from a player whose poster once adorned your bedroom wall, it somehow rekindles a kindred spirit, a long-lost connection with both the player and your own childhood. Players from days gone by tend to be far more approachable and will always have time for the fans of the clubs they played for.

Now, City weren't exactly setting the world alight in 1983, and after declaring myself a Blue I received some serious abuse from schoolmates who just couldn't get the heads around why I'd chosen Manchester City, refusing to believe I had a relative who played for the club. I was totally obsessed with City, which virtually took over my life. Unfortunately, there was hardly any media coverage of City at this time, and even less when we were in the old Second Division, so I'd often have to get the latest news by scrolling through Teletext or by ringing the City ClubCall line. One day I returned home from school to find that the TV and video were missing from my bedroom. My mum had sold them off to pay for the massive phone bill that I'd run up.

I first got my chance to see City play live in November 1985, away at Luton Town, only half an hour from our home in Milton Keynes. Manchester to me in those days was just a place I dreamt of visiting, and Maine Road seemed a world away. After many months of badgering my parents to take me, they finally gave in. My mum kitted me out from head to toe in knitted blue and white City colours, and I couldn't have been prouder on my way to watch the Blues. The walk to the ground felt amazing and we entered the first turnstile we saw. Off came the coat to reveal my full get-up; but after a few minutes of dirty looks we could tell something wasn't right. As the chants of "City, City" went up from the far end of the ground it dawned on us that we were in the wrong end, and needed to move – quickly. It was a traumatic experience for a ten-year-old when the stewards promptly threw us out, and my dad was seething as we headed back to the van to go straight home. I was distraught, but he finally saw sense and we headed back to the ground where he had to pay again at the right turnstile. Again, I was instantly hooked. The atmosphere in that tiny away end was electric and I couldn't help but watch the many characters I was surrounded by. Everyone seemed to know each other, and I desperately wanted to be part of it. For the record, we lost 2-1 that day – Typical City!

One the most enjoyable aspects of collecting, for me, is the groundwork that goes into finding a shirt, or the thrill of unearthing a rarity. Always look for a shirt in the least expected place you'd ever think of finding one. If you don't ask, then you don't get. That's the number one rule.

I'm sure I speak for all collectors when I say that opening a random online message that starts with the words, "I have this shirt if you're interested in it" – and then the shirt

turning out to be a real treasure – provides a unique buzz. I was contacted recently with that exact message, asking "did I think the shirt was genuine?" It turned out to be the long-sleeve chequered away shirt issued to Mick McCarthy for the 1986/87 season, which was used just seven times in that campaign – though not by Mick, as he refused to wear long-sleeved shirts. It had been given to a young City fan by his next-door neighbour who used to work in the Maine Road laundry room!

A question I'm often asked is about the favourite shirt in my collection. It's difficult, given the number to choose from, but at the moment it's a 1967/68 Colin Bell Umbro home shirt worn

by arguably City's greatest ever player, during a title-winning season.

One that runs it close is a more modern shirt from an equally great player in David Silva, worn in City's match against Watford in September 2019 during City's 125th anniversary celebrations. The shirt was a gift from City as a 'thank you' for displaying eleven shirts from the collection in a mock-up dressing room at CitySquare entertainment before the match. I was asked to drop off the shirts at reception, but had to explain that while I was more than happy to bring the shirts, there was no way I would be leaving their side! My lad and I spent a fantastic couple of hours

meeting and chatting with fellow Blues and giving them a bit a history behind the shirts – while keeping a close eye on the kids with burgers and drinks in hand approaching them! I was asked if we'd like our seats upgraded to the Legends Lounge as a thank you, but instead I had a cheeky idea in mind, asking for a shirt of the greatest City player I've seen in my time watching the Blues. The CitySquare matchday manager said she'd ask, but that it would be very unlikely. Ah, well. If you don't ask, you don't get...

Once the display was finished and the shirts were safely packed away, we sat back and enjoyed a stunning 8-0 City win, captained by Silva who just happened to open the scoring in the first minute of the match. I'd completely forgotten I'd even asked 'that' shirt question as we made our way back to Piccadilly for the train journey home, which was then interrupted by a phone call. It was the lady at CitySquare, informing me that my request had been granted – and could I please make my way to the CityHome office to pick up the shirt that was waiting for me? It was the quickest half-mile dash I've ever made, to collect the shirt fresh from Merlin's back, still completely wet through. And the first thing I did was – yes, you've guessed it – sniff the shirt!

As far as the future is concerned for my collection, I certainly don't see any signs of it slowing down as yet. I have a certain target in mind for a number of shirts to reach. Well, every man does need a hobby...

Georgeeorge Hicks's shirt from the second of City's 11 FA Cup final appearances, against Bolton Wanderers on 26th April 1926.

City adopted a darker blue, known as 'cornflower blue', for the final. Unfortunately the shirt's coat-of-arms badge has been carefully removed at some stage.

Outside-left Hicks played a key role on City's journey to Wembley, scoring six times, but was unable to prevent the Blues going down 1-0 in front of 91,000 fans.

One of my all-time favourite shirt finds... Billy Sowden's matchworn jersey from the evening of 14th October 1953 – a landmark friendly match that finished City 6-3 Heart of Midlothian. The shirt had lain safely in the same Manchester chest of drawers for 66 years before it was finally added to the collection.

Reserve centre-forward Sowden became the first player to score under Maine Road's new floodlights, which made their debut that autumn night – and promptly went on to claim a hat-trick in the game. But he never did take Don Revie's first-team place.

The Umbro design was a special one-off made from shiny, silky material to help players pick each other out under the lights, which were hugely atmospheric but not the brightest by today's standards.

Floodlit friendlies then became a regular attraction, with City playing nine in total throughout the 1953/54 season, including games against other Scottish sides, Celtic and East Fife.

13

This unnumbered spare match shirt from the 1956 FA Cup final is a fantastic Umbro design, used just once for City's sixth and surely most iconic Wembley visit.

The shirt was a birthday gift to a young City fan from a member of the club's backroom staff, and has been stored in pristine condition ever since.

City would take the Cup back to Manchester after a 3-1 victory over Birmingham City in a game now referred to as the 'Trautmann Final' after City's legendary German keeper, who played out the final 17 minutes with a broken neck following a collision with Birmingham's Peter Murphy.

The final was also unique for one other reason: referee Alf Bond only had one arm.

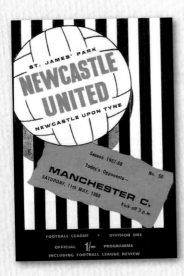

Colin Bell's 1967/68 First Division matchworn shirt. 'The King' would appear 35 times in the League that season, scoring 14 times wearing this iconic number eight shirt.

City clinched the First Division title on the final day of the season with a dramatic 4-3 victory over Newcastle United in Colin's home town. It was enough to seal our first top-flight title for 31 years, beating rivals United to the crown by two points.

Just eleven days later, the inspirational midfielder won his England call-up, claiming the first of his 48 caps in a 3-1 friendly win over Sweden at Wembley Stadium. Bell's international career would have been far longer if not for the cataclysmic knee injury sustained in a 1975 League Cup tie.

This shirt was originally given by Tommy Booth to a fellow Blue as a gift for his son, who was close friends with the family. Fast-forward to 2018, and the lucky recipient kindly decided to auction off the shirt via Twitter to help raise vital treatment funds for Isla Caton, a young girl who is still bravely battling neuroblastoma.

Once City were aware of the story, they generously offered the shirt donor and winning bidder two Tunnel Club seats for the Champions' League fixture against Hoffenheim. I was delighted to win the shirt and duly transferred the amount direct to Isla's family.

What followed was a fantastic night at City with my son Harvey, meeting the Blue who put the shirt up for auction, having actually worn it himself to a few games! It was presented to me by Tommy himself, and we spent a great night in the company of legends such as Bell, Summerbee and Barnes.

Then Harvey was treated to a trip to the dressing room where he was given match shirts by Sterling and Laporte. The night reduced me to tears, and those who know me and Harvey's story will understand why. What a shirt, and what an amazing night City gave us.

Willie Donachie's home shirt, worn throughout the 1973/74 First Division campaign which saw the departure of bosses Johnny Hart and Ron Saunders.

The popular Scottish defender appeared over 430 times for the Blues during a ten-year spell, and later returned to the club as assistant manager under Joe Royle.

Originally a gift from Willie's father to a family of Blues.

A very stylish City away shirt featuring eye-catching sash, Umbro diamond trim and coat-of-arms badge with 1976/77 League Runners-up embroidery. The gull wing-collared shirt was used for three seasons in all, up to 1978/79.

The great Dennis Tueart bagged a glorious hat-trick wearing this very shirt during City's 4-1 away win over Ron Saunders' Aston Villa on 24th August 1977.

One of the greatest of all City players, Colin Bell made his final appearance wearing his famous number eight shirt on 10th February 1979, against Manchester United. Then just short of his 33rd birthday, he had never recovered from a terrible knee injury sustained against United three seasons earlier, though he did manage six more games wearing the unfamiliar number six.

The shirt is signed by Bell, and was presented by the man himself to a match official following his testimonial fixture on 11th September 1979, when a combined Manchester XI beat a Merseyside XI by two goals to one.

'The King' signed for City from Bury in March 1966 for £45,000, then a record fee for a teenager. Within 48 hours he had made a goal-scoring debut in a 2-1 win at Derby County as City stormed towards the Second Division title.

Over the course of his 13-year career with City Bell won First and Second Division championship medals, FA Cup and League Cup winner's medals and a European Cup Winners' Cup medal.

He made a total of 393 League appearances with a handsome return of 119 goals.

Brian Kidd wore this shirt in a UEFA Cup second-round meeting with Standard Liège in Belgium, in October 1978.

He swapped it with a Liège defender at the end of the second-leg fixture. Although the Blues went down 2-0 on the night, they progressed 4-2 on aggregate following a first-leg Maine Road victory with goals from Kidd (2), Roger Palmer and Asa Hartford.

With Big Joe missing from 1979/80's end-of-season tour fixtures due to an England call-up, City drafted in Oldham keeper John Platt on loan.

Prior to the tour Corrigan had been ever present throughout the 42-game League campaign, wearing this very shirt. However, it was John rather than Joe who claimed the right to swap the shirt with Roma defender Luciano Spinosi following City's 3-2 victory in Italy.

Interestingly, 1979/80 was the first season that Umbro introduced nylon shirts for the outfield players; but Joe somehow managed to negotiate himself this traditional, thick cotton design – perhaps better suited for diving around in the Maine Road goalmouths' muddy puddles.

Joe's first-team tenure at City spanned 1967-83, and on his watch we won the European Cup Winners' Cup and two League Cups. He is still a charismatic, larger-than-life figure at the club on matchday hospitality duties.

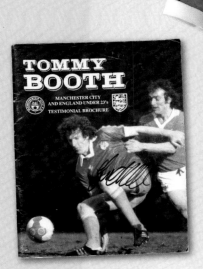

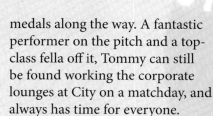

Tommy Booth's shirt from his own testimonial match in May 1981, when the team from City's recent FA Cup final appearance took on the 1969 FA Cup final side.

The Middleton-born stopper appeared over 380 times for his boyhood club between 1967 and 1981, winning a host of medals along the way. A fantastic performer on the pitch and a top-class fella off it, Tommy can still be found working the corporate lounges at City on a matchday, and always has time for everyone.

Just for the record, Tommy's '69 Old Boys suffered an unlucky 9-2 reversal on his big day!

The spare shirt, also known as the 'blood shirt', from the 1981 FA Cup semi-final versus Ipswich Town.

It has all the player features you'd expect, with the woven nylon material design that City employed from 1979-81, and the coat-of-arms badge.

It was Paul Power's stunning extra-time free-kick winner at Villa Park that earned City's passage to our first Wembley FA Cup final since 1969.

Umbro introduced this silk-style shirt for 1981/82, which proved to be the last season that City players ran out without the accompaniment of a shirt sponsor. This long-sleeved number ten home shirt was worn by both Tommy Hutchison and Asa Hartford during a comfortable mid-season campaign.

Hutchison was the first new recruit of John Bond's reign as City manager, and will be forever remembered in City folklore as the player who scored at both ends in the 1981 FA Cup final.

31

CAN TURN FASTER THAN
NEIL McNAB

The Saab 900 Turbo has its own distinctive character on the road – a bit like Neil McNab, exciting and fast but at the same time utterly reliable and safe.
The car is always in perfect co-ordination with the driver and responds immediately and accurately, to the driver's actions. Even with a full load the car is consistent in its behaviour in unexpected situations.
Take a test drive in a Saab 900 Turbo at any of the four dealers listed below and turn faster than Neil McNab!

SAAB
& CITY

Shirt sponsorship arrived at Maine Road in the 1982/83 season, with Swedish car manufacturers Saab putting their name across the players' chests.

The lettering was changed from black to white on the home shirts at the request of Saab in early October as they believed it would stand out more.

This number ten shirt was worn by Asa Hartford during his second spell at the club.

TOUGH AS
MICK McCARTHY

When it comes to toughness there's few that can compare with City's exciting new acquisition, Mick McCarthy.
As tough as the premier range of cars produced by City's latest new house.
Manufactured to perform at the best in all conditions, each head up displays a strength which not only protects the long lasting bodywork but also ensures the safety of the car's most valued asset – the passengers.
Tell big Mick that toughness is only a part of the story. Understand the essential there is a styling of sheer performance of its own.
We know in City, Mick, it's in one tough guy to another.

SAAB
& CITY

SPRINGFIELD

SCENE
THE OFFICIAL
PROGRAMME
OF WIGAN
ATHLETIC 40p

Tuesday, 5th October, 1982 — Kick-off 7.45 p.m.
MILK CUP, SECOND ROUND, FIRST LEG
WIGAN ATHLETIC -v- MANCHESTER CITY
Tonight's Match is sponsored by WIMPEY HOMES

Asa Hartford's matchworn shirt from 5th October 1982, when City drew 1-1 at Wigan in the Milk Cup second round.

It was the only time the shirt with paired stripes was worn during the 1982/83 relegation season as Saab ditched the black-coloured logo shortly after, leaving City to continue with a sponsor-free away shirt for the rest of the campaign.

The black 'SAAB' lettering would reappear on the shirt during the 1983/84 season in Division Two.

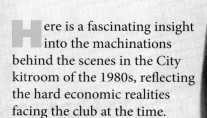

Here is a fascinating insight into the machinations behind the scenes in the City kitroom of the 1980s, reflecting the hard economic realities facing the club at the time.

In today's Premier League era, when every City player appears to have an almost infinite number of shirts at their disposal to to swap with opposition players and give away to fans, the idea of first-team shirts being recycled for further use seems every bit as out of date as the age of darning socks by hand on a wooden mushroom.

However, here is the 1983/84 long-sleeved home number 14 shirt with the white Saab logo, which shows distinct evidence of repurposing when City's sponsorship deal switched to Philips at the season's end.

In fact, the first-team's Saab shirts were then donated down to the 1984/85 Youth team, who continued to use the kit with the addition of the new sponsor's name on a sizeable patch stitched over the former incumbent's logo.

This shirt was a gift from City legend Ken Barnes to YTS player Sean Harkin as a birthday treat.

Derek Parlane enjoyed a successful debut season in the Second Division wearing this Saab-sponsored jersey. The sharp-shooting Scotsman appeared 43 times in all competitions, scoring 19 goals during 1983/84.

Sadly, his time at Maine Road was to be brief as boss Billy McNeill continued a high-turnover policy – of strikers in particular – juggling the pack as the Blues strived for a return to First Division football.

During his tenure from 1983 to 1986 the ex-Celtic legend tried out a total of 12 forwards in his ever-changing front line. Through the revolving door with Parlane came Steve Kinsey, Duncan Davidson, Gordon Dalziel, David Johnson, Gordon Smith, Darren Beckford, Jim Melrose, Tony Cunningham, Gordon Davies, Mark Lillis, Paul Moulden and Trevor Christie.

City clinched promotion back to the First Division with a stunning 5-1 victory over Charlton Athletic on 11th May 1985, in front of a packed, roasting-hot Maine Road. And it was Paul Simpson who scored the glorious fourth, wearing this very shirt.

Going into the final day, City's run-in under Billy McNeill had seriously derailed with just two wins in the previous ten games, and now key players such as Nicky Reid, Clive Wilson and Mick McCarthy were missing through suspension and injury.

Young 'Simmo' proved to be a real star of the show during the run-in, scoring six goals in City's final eight fixtures, paving the way for City's return to Division One after a two-season absence.

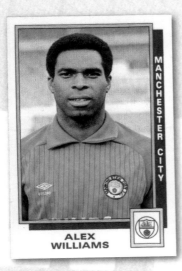

ALEX
WILLIAMS

Following an injury to long-time City keeper Joe Corrigan, 19-year-old Alex Williams made his City bow on Saturday 14th March 1981 in a 2-1 Maine Road win over West Brom.

The popular Moss Sider went on to cement his place as City's number one following the sale of Corrigan in 1983, gaining England Youth and Under-21 honours along the way.

Big Alex was an ever-present throughout City's great 1984/85 promotion season, before injury put paid to what had been a highly promising career. A loan spell at Queen of the South and a move to Port Vale ensued, but he knew deep down that he couldn't maintain the high standards he'd previously set, and was forced to retire in September 1987.

Alex continued to work behind the scenes at City, and in 2002 received an MBE for services to young people. He's still heavily involved on matchdays, and with City's amazing CITC team.

The 1986 Full Members' Cup final shirt proved one of the most difficult of the decade to obtain for the collection.

Graham Baker replaced Nicky Reid in the 58th minute of the inaugural final against Chelsea, where the lads went down 5-4 in a thriller, having been asked to play at Wembley just 24 hours after getting a draw in the Manchester derby at Old Trafford.

The shirt is the 1984-86 away shirt design which had the coat-of-arms badge heat-pressed on for use in the final only. Replica shirts were available to buy from the souvenir shop with the same badge applied, although the players' shirts have a white fleece lining.

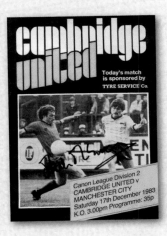

Canon League Division 2
CAMBRIDGE UNITED v
MANCHESTER CITY
Saturday 17th December 1983
K.O. 3.00pm Programme: 35p

'm often asked about the favourite shirt in my collection, so here it is... Mick McCarthy's matchworn shirt from 1985-87.

I've already shared the 'genesis story' of my shirt collection, so it's a special feeling to reveal my very first player-worn shirt which set my obsession in motion.

As you now know, it was thanks to the unique combination of my Grandad Danny and my cousin Mick that I became a Blue.

I only ever set out to find one matchworn shirt that had belonged to Mick; but there was probably a precursor that hinted at the way my collection might go. Way back when my grandad first mentioned Mick's fantastic career move, he subsequently produced a small pile of City home match programmes, most of which were signed to me by the entire City first team.

I was hooked. Now I had a real focus in life. CITY. I truly believe you don't choose to follow City: they're either chosen for you or City choose you. My story could have been so very different had Mick been tempted by potential moves to Newcastle or Sheff Wed from his hometown club, Barnsley. For the record, Mick made his City debut away at Cambridge United on Saturday 17th December 1983.

This wonderful Umbro home shirt, complete with silky finish and wrapover collar, proved a real favourite design with the City faithful.

Over the course of its two seasons in use, this historic number nine jersey – autographed personally for me by Gordon Davies – was also worn in First Division matches by his fellow strikers Steve Kinsey, Trevor Christie and Imre Varadi.

Umbro's chequered design for the 1986/87 away shirt was considered daring at the time.

This matchworn number seven, with its extra-large 'PHILIPS' sponsor logo, was worn by Gordon Davies, Robert Hopkins, David White and Andy May.

The shirt only had a lifespan of a single campaign, before Philips were replaced as sponsors by Brother Industries.

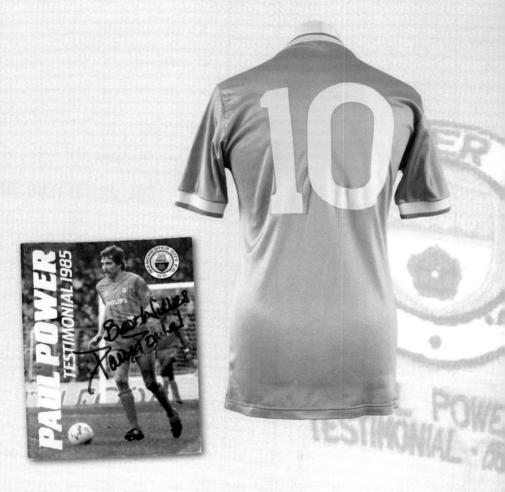

The shirt worn by Clive Wilson in Paul Power's richly deserved 1985 testimonial match.

After eleven years as a Blue – and 36 goals in 445 appearances – Power was snapped up by Everton boss Howard Kendall for a mere £65,000 in June 1986. But he returned just a few months later for his testimonial fixture against his new club, playing 45 minutes for each side as the Merseysiders ran out 4-1 winners.

Originally signed as cover by Kendall, he would go on to play a starring role for the Toffees which saw him win a First Division winner's medal, scoring at Maine Road in a 3-1 Everton win but refusing to celebrate his goal.

brother
the future at your fingertips.

MANCHESTER CITY
V HUDDERSFIELD TOWN

SATURDAY 7TH NOVEMBER 1987
KICK-OFF 3:00PM
BARCLAYS LEAGUE DIVISION TWO

Admission price (including VAT)	You are advised to take up your position half an hour before the kick-off.	ROW M
£ 4.50	J.B. HALFORD Secretary	SEAT 217

MANCHESTER CITY F.C. PLC
MAINE ROAD, MOSS SIDE, MANCHESTER
TO BE RETAINED

Steve Redmond, the young City skipper, was ever present in all competitions in 1987/88, including the historic 10-1 victory over Huddersfield Town, where three players scored hat-tricks and David White was presented with this Mitre match ball.

The captain of City's 1986 FA Youth Cup winning team, Redmond made his first-team debut on 8th February 1986 against QPR. He was one of seven members of the FAYC squad who made the leap to the big time, along with Ian Brightwell, Paul Lake, Andy Hinchcliffe, Ian Scott, David White and Paul Moulden.

Steve's quilted-effect shirt features the short-lived white Umbro logo which would change to black for the 1988/89 season.

Kenny Clements 1987/88 Division Two

In the second season City sported the red and black chequered away shirt it saw the addition of not just the new club sponsor's logo but also stylish lines of piping to the shoulders and arms.

The number four shirt was mainly worn by Kenny Clements (8 times) but also got run-outs courtesy of Mark Seagraves (4), Paul Lake (2) and Neil McNab (1) during its only season.

Often referred to as the 'deckchair' shirt by City supporters, this candy-striped number eight was worn by Paul Moulden, Trevor Morley and Paul Lake on the road during the 1988/89 Second Division promotion season. It would reappear at the start of the following First Division campaign before being replaced by a darker maroon away shirt.

Ahh, the great unwashed! Here is Trevor Morley's authentically mucky matchworn shirt from City's glorious promotion-clinching game away at Bradford City's Valley Parade on the last day of the 1988/89 season.

In the 86th minute, Morley miraculously converted a David White cross on a quick counter-attack to secure a 1-1 draw and City's return to Division One.

At the whistle, inflatable-fuelled mayhem ensued on the pitch.

A new Umbro design with innovative shadow weave marked City's return to the First Division under Mel Machin.

Skipper Brian Gayle's appearances included the 'Maine Road Massacre', when Manchester United were thrashed 5-1.

Gayle then fell out of favour and was replaced by Scottish defensive ace Colin Hendry. 'Braveheart' took over the number five shirt on his debut at home to Nottingham Forest on November 18th 1989 – when he was voted Man of the Match despite a 3-0 defeat.

59

arly away games in 1989/90 had seen City in maroon and white stripes. For the trip to Highbury on October 14th, blue home shirts were expected, but a shorts clash saw City opt for an all-yellow strip originally designed by Umbro to be used on New Year's Day 1990 at Sheffield Wednesday.

Blurry-eyed travelling Blues were left staring in disbelief as we trotted out in banana yellow: the last time City had worn a yellow shirt had been at nearby Spurs, back in the 1960/61 season.

After a 4-0 thumping, rumour had it that club chairman Peter Swales had ordered the kit to be burned. In fact, it was donated by director Freddie Pye to a Sunday league side called MMS. Only one set of 15 shirts was produced, becoming the holy grail of City match shirts for collectors.

A real jewel in the collection, all thanks to top Blue, Billy Bell.

Another hugely popular early-'90s design, Umbro's maroon shadow-woven away shirt was used for two seasons, including the final campaign before the introduction of the Premier League.

This particular jersey was worn by full-back Neil Pointon on 19th October 1991 in a 1-0 victory at Tottenham. It was then gifted by Neil to Blues fan Steven Holmes upon the team's arrival back at Maine Road. After many years stored away, it was kindly donated into the collection. Thanks Steven, it's finally found a perfect home!

An ultra-rare white third shirt, complete with Football League arm badges, as worn by Alan Harper and Gary Megson during its only season in use. A keenly sought style for collectors of both matchworn and replica shirts.

The full set of kit was donated to the City in the Community football team who used it for a number years for five-a-sides and friendly fixtures, which saw many of the shirts being lost or worn out and thrown away over time.

1992/93's inaugural FA Premier League season saw David White sporting the new button-up home shirt with shadow weave and sleeve stripes.

It's interesting to note that the squad numbers and player names usually associated with the Premier League didn't actually appear until its second season, when the PL sleeve badges changed from plastic to a more durable cotton style.

White scored City's landmark first Premier League goal in this shirt, and went on to be an ever-present in Peter Reid's side.

This was also the last time he ever appeared wearing number 32, as he would switch to his more favoured number eleven for the start of the 1994/95 campaign.

Blues fans will recall the Wednesday fixture on the final day of the season as the time that the 'Uwe Rosler' chant really took off, sung consistently throughout the game in baking hot May sunshine. Beagrie assisted Rosler for City's only goal in a 1-1 draw.

Peter Beagrie only wore this purple (it's a long, long way from maroon) striped Umbro away shirt on one occasion, and that was against Sheffield Wednesday on 7th May 1994.

The early 1990s saw the trend for third shirts take off at many Premier League clubs. City introduced this white and black striped jersey at the start of the 1993/94 season, and it remained in use for two campaigns.

As you can see – though only just, as the kitman nearly ran out of space – this particular shirt was worn by David Brightwell in a 0-0 draw at Boundary Park, Oldham on 26th March 1994.

Brightwell was a product of City's Youth side, and had made his first-team debut at Wimbledon in February 1992. He went on to appear over 40 times for the club before departing for Bradford City in 1995.

Andy Dibble 1994/95 Premier League

The rather lairy yellow and purple striped keeper jersey was most often worn by Tony Coton in 1994/95, and just once by Andy Dibble on 22nd October 1994. The occasion was City's 5-2 thrashing of Spurs at Maine Road, widely regarded as manager Brian Horton's finest result.

The fixture was originally dubbed 'The Clash of the Germans', with Uwe Rosler and Jurgen Klinnsman expected to hit the headlines; but sadly Rosler missed the match through injury.

The shirt was a late replacement made by Umbro to avoid a nightmarish kit clash with Tottenham goalie Ian Walker.

Dibble's shirt was kindly donated into the collection by fellow Blues Patrick and David Moran.

David Rocastle made his City debut in this shirt in the Premier League clash with Southampton on 28th December 1993, then wore it once more at Newcastle before switching to the long-sleeved version.

It's the first in a series of shirts seemingly designed to suggest an undershirt is being worn. The Umbro tape around the bottom of the sleeves is more subtle than the giant diamond logo shadow weave.

David made 23 appearances in his only season with City before moving on to Chelsea in the summer of 1994. Following his departure, the number seven shirt remained vacant until the arrival of Georgi Kinkladze at the start of the 1995/96 campaign.

Midfielder Rocastle is perhaps best remembered for the seven great years he spent with Arsenal before joining City via Leeds United. Tragically, he was later diagnosed with non-Hodgkin's lymphoma and passed away aged just 33 in 2001. RIP 'Rocky'.

Paul Walsh pulled on this shirt for City's Premier League match at Sheffield Wednesday on 17th September 1994.

The black and red away shirt was used over two seasons, the first appearance of this traditional striped style since 1984/85 – although it now featured an additional mesh-effect chest panel.

Tricky striker Walsh, an inspired deadline-day signing by Brian Horton in March 1994, enjoyed a career purple patch with City before returning to Portsmouth in a swap deal involving Kit Symons and Gerry Creaney – an unpopular exchange for many Blues fans.

GEORGI KINKLADZE

The shirt with the 'CITY' shadow weave worn by Georgi Kinkladze in his final Premier League appearance, v Liverpool on 5th May 1996. Showing clear signs of having been patched up, the jersey was earlier ripped but repaired in time for Gio's 'Goal of the Season' against Southampton.

The mesmeric Georgian was first spotted showing off his skills in an international fixture against Wales and, despite strong interest from big European clubs, it was rumoured that chairman Francis Lee secured a first-option deal.

Sadly, 'Kinky's debut 1995/96 season at City ended in relegation, as did his third and final campaign. No third-tier performer, Georgi departed for Ajax for £5 million in the summer of 1998.

The shirt was given to fellow Blue Liam Flynn by Kinkladze after the Liverpool game, and then remained, unwashed, hanging in Liam's wardrobe for the little matter of 27 years.

Designed by Umbro for the 1995/96 campaign, the local manufacturer would have to wait 14 years before the chance to produce another City kit.

Alas, this would be Niall Quinn's last season with the club. Having arrived from Arsenal in March 1990, the big Irish target man exited for Sunderland in the wake of City's devastating relegation on the last day of the season, when a 2-2 draw at home to Liverpool proved too little, too late.

Following his withdrawal from the game, Quinn could be seen running down the touchline screaming at team-mates that we needed another goal to survive after false information had filtered through to the players that a draw would be enough to keep us up.

Of the two shirt styles available to players, Quinn favoured the short-sleeved version, only ever appearing once in this long-sleeved jersey.

UMBRO

brother

MANCHESTER CITY
F.C.

7

Following on the family trade in the footsteps of legendary City flanker Mike, Summerbee Jr joined City from Swindon Town during 1994, joining Brian Horton's attacking line-up alongside Beagrie, Rosler and Walsh.

Following the appointment of Alan Ball, and relegation from the PL in 1996, Summerbee joined former Blues boss Peter Reid at Sunderland in a deal that brought Craig Russell to Maine Road.

Umbro's maroon and white 'half-and-half' sash style was worn by City in just seven fixtures in its only season before it was handed down to the Youth team – and winger Nicky Summerbee appeared in every match.

City really broke from tradition with a switch to Kappa in July 1997. In the mid to late '90s the Italian manufacturers were fast becoming a big name in world kits, producing for the likes of Juventus and Barcelona.

The 'laser blue' home shirt caused many a raised eyebrow among fans, with 'MCFC' applied across the rear, and it now carries painful memories of relegation to the third tier on the final day of 1997/98, despite a 5-2 victory at Stoke City.

The appearance of Kappa logos down the sleeves was the first revival of the style since 1980/81, when Umbro's diamonds featured.

The number eleven shirt was worn by Uwe Rosler, Paul Dickov and Ged Brannan.

Kappa's maroon-hooped blue and white half-and-half away shirt from City's calamitous 1997/98 Nationwide League Division One relegation season. Mercifully, it was only worn three times, at Ipswich, Crewe and Stockport – though it did also make appearances (minus the Nationwide sleeve badges) in pre-season friendly matches against Burnley and Falkirk.

This shirt was worn by Eddie McGoldrick in his final City appearance, away to Stockport County on 29th November 1997.

Kevin Horlock   1997/98 Division One

Kevin Horlock's matchworn shirt from the Nationwide League Division One match against QPR on 26th October 1997 – a 2-0 reversal under Frank Clark.

The elusive, asymmetric-striped Kappa third shirt was only worn on four other occasions, versus Portsmouth, Huddersfield Town, Reading and Birmingham City.

It was never available to buy as a replica, and it is rumoured that only a single set of shirts was ever produced for the club.

MANCHESTER CITY'S 1998/99 SEASON

What an impact Big Andy Morrison had on our fateful 1998/99 season, giving City a vital shot in the arm just when we'd hit our lowest ever point in our only campaign to date in the third tier of English football.

Signed by Joe Royle for £80,000 from Huddersfield, the Scottish central stopper was instantly made captain, scored the winner on his debut and never looked back. Our saviour, a true cult hero.

Andy's Play-off shirt was swapped with Gillingham's Paul Smith following the melodramatic, now-iconic Wembley final, and was then purchased direct from Smith by a fellow collector who actually visited the Gillingham training ground to ask the players about the swapped shirts.

It next changed hands with a few collectors before being eventually sold on to me by a dealer who was selling up his City collection.

I asked Andy, now a City ambassador on matchdays, to sign the back of the shirt for me, and he then made me promise to give him first refusal should the shirt ever become available. You have my word, Skipper. The shirt is yours, should it ever be moved on.

haun Goater's shirt from the 1999 Division Two Play-off final is unusual for two reasons: firstly 'The Goat' was issued with two short-sleeved shirts, according to his preference, rather than the usual choice of short and long; also, it was only worn during the first half of the match, as he changed his shirt at half-time due to the heavy rain.

The burly Bermudan endured a rocky start to his City career, but 103 goals in a five-year stay firmly cemented Goater's place in the hearts of every Blues fan. His personal roll of honour includes three promotions, top-scorer status four seasons in a row and the landmark of being the first City player to hit more than 30 goals in a single season ever since Franny Lee back in 1972.

'Feed The Goat' and he would certainly score.

Tony Vaughan   1999 Play-Off Final

ony Vaughan came on as a sub in the 1999 Wembley Play-off final, replacing skipper Andy Morrison in the 61st minute. But his number 13 long-sleeved shirt proved anything but unlucky.

The shirt comes unwashed, complete with authentic Wembley mud stains, direct from Gillingham's Mark Saunders who swapped jerseys after City's amazing, last-gasp victory.

Manchester born Vaughan was a product of the City youth set-up before heading off to join the Ipswich Town academy. However, manager Frank Clark brought Tony back home during the summer of 1997 in £1.35 million deal, and he stayed for two seasons before joining Nottingham Forest. He will always be appreciated by the City faithful for his endeavours during our only season in the third tier of English football.

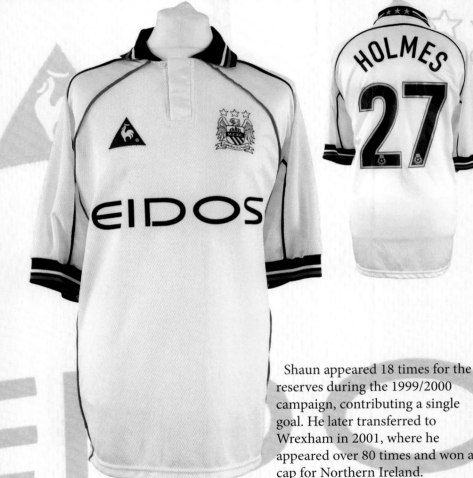

Shaun appeared 18 times for the reserves during the 1999/2000 campaign, contributing a single goal. He later transferred to Wrexham in 2001, where he appeared over 80 times and won a cap for Northern Ireland.

This was the first of eight away shirts designed by Le Coq Sportif. It was used in just six fixtures during the season: at Burnley (League Cup), Ipswich, Birmingham, Crystal Palace, Barnsley and Portsmouth.

Another of City's 'one-season wonder' away shirts, which was designed by Le Coq Sportif and issued to left-back Shaun Holmes who kindly donated the jersey into the collection.

Robert Taylor is remembered as the man who almost broke City hearts at the Wembley Play-off final in 1999, when he scored Gillingham's second goal; and then he helped repair them in May 2000 with a vital goal against Birmingham City as City returned to Premier League football after a four-year absence.

The tough, free-scoring centre-forward was signed by Joe Royle during City's second successive promotion season, though Robert chose to move on to Wolves for personal reasons without ever showing us his obvious goalscoring abilities. His shirt was worn in City's pre-season friendly with Ireland's Drogheda United on 24th July 2000.

Fiery Australian full-back Danny Tiatto appeared 35 times in the 1999/2000 season, which saw Joe Royle's side clinch a return to the Premier League after a four-year absence.

Tiatto enjoyed a six-year spell with City, over which time he became one of a select band of 12 players who have worn the shirt in three tiers of English football.

The other seats on the City rollercoaster belonged to Nicky Weaver, Richard Edghill, Gerard Wiekens, Andy Morrison, Michael Brown, Ian Bishop, Kevin Horlock, Shaun Goater, Paul Dickov, Jeff Whitley and Lee Crooks.

Former World Player of the Year George Weah was an exciting, big-name signing in August 2000, all set for City's return to the Premier League; but just eleven games and four goals later, he was gone. After a few appearances it was clear that George was now lacking his legendary pace and fire, and sadly he never did form a partnership with Paulo Wanchope.

Instead, he had a bust-up with boss Joe Royle and claimed he had been "treated like a child." Having later entered politics, in 2018 Weah was elected President of Liberia.

Le Coq Sportif's V-neck, red and black third shirt is one of the hardest to find from this era, especially as examples from the three seasons of use are split by featuring either Football League or Premier League sleeve badges.

This shirt was a gift from City midfielder Alf-Inge Haaland to a Norwegian supporter who had travelled to the UK especially to watch the League Cup game at Gillingham on 26th September 2000 – a 4-2 extra-time thriller.

A real rarity from City's 2001/02 Nationwide League promotion season – the silver alternate keeper jersey was only ever used twice. On each occasion, this shirt was bench-worn by Carlo Nash, at Newcastle in the FA Cup and in the Coventry home League fixture. The shirt was never available to buy as a replica.

Steve Howey's matchworn shirt from the successful League Division One campaign.

The central defender appeared 38 times for the yoyo-ing Blues, scoring three goals from the backline (he notched up a useful eleven overall) as Kevin Keegan's men clinched the title and an automatic return to the top tier.

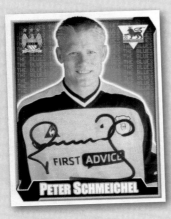

FIRST ADVICE

PETER SCHMEICHEL

SCHMEICHEL

1

Following City's return to the Premier League in 2002, manager Kevin Keegan shocked many Blues when he picked up Danish keeper Peter Schmeichel on a free transfer following his release from Aston Villa.

Schmeichel would go on to make 31 appearances in his last season as a professional, including the last ever Maine Road derby, where City overcame his former side 3-1.

'The Great Dane' also gave a starring performance in a 2-1 Anfield win and appeared in the historic landmark of the last competitive fixture played at Maine Road. Sad to say the game was lost 1-0 to Southampton.

The regular City goalkeeper jersey for the 2002/03 season was yellow with black shoulders and sleeves. This blue and green alternate colourway was worn by Schmeichel against Leeds United on 11th January 2003.

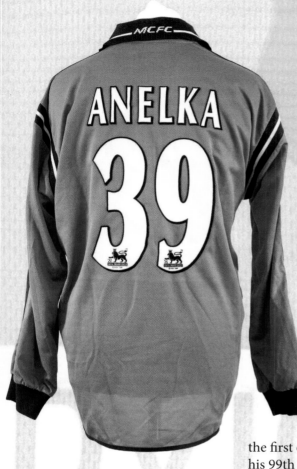

The last League 'derby' to be played at Maine Road

to shake hands in the tunnel before the match with City captain Peter Schmeichel; but perhaps even more for Neville's tidy assist for the first of two Shaun Goater goals, his 99th and 100th for the club. Great work all round.

After the game, the shirt was gifted by the French striker to award-winning photographer and lifelong City supporter Kevin Cummins, who spent the season producing a book based around the club's 80th and final year at Maine Road.

Nicolas Anelka's matchworn shirt from the last ever Manchester derby at Maine Road, on November 7th 2002. Anelka scored City's first goal in our first Derby Day win for 13 years.

The richly symbolic win is also fondly remembered for United full-back Gary Neville's refusal

How welcome it was when the designers at Le Coq Sportif provided City with this away shirt referencing the unusual sash styles last worn by the club's players in the late '70s.

Israeli international Berkovic was signed from Celtic in July 2001 by new City manager Kevin Keegan. Eyal formed a brilliant partnership with Ali Benarbi as Blues bounced straight back to the PL.

Marc-Vivien Foé hit two goals in City's 3-1 Boxing Day victory over Aston Villa in 2002. After the game he generously gave his shirt as a gift to the daughter of a well-known Blues supporter.

The hugely popular Cameroon international spent the season at City, on loan from Lyon. He scored nine League goals, including City's last ever goal at Maine Road.

But just two months later the football world was shocked by Foé's sudden passing following an on-field collapse playing for his country against Colombia in Lyon.

A nother well-judged reference to an iconic past City shirt, Le Coq Sportif's update of the 1956 FA Cup final colours was only used twice in the course of its single season, 2002/03.

This shirt was worn on the bench by Darren Huckerby at West Bromwich Albion on 2nd November 2002. The wing ace was signed by Joe Royle in December 2000 as the Blues battled the drop, then he enjoyed a fantastic 2001/02 campaign, netting 26 times as City bounced straight back to the big league under Kevin Keegan.

Here is the Reebok goalkeeper jersey worn by David Seaman on his City debut, in the UEFA Cup match against Total Network Solutions on 14th August 2003.

The shirt was subsequently swapped after the match with TNS keeper Gerald Doherty.

Perhaps surprisingly, in the 2003/04 tournament, UEFA allowed no sleeve patches or logos on the numbers of players' shirts.

After Peter Schmeichel's decision to retire at the end of the 2002/03 campaign, Kevin Keegan opted again for an experienced, big-name keeper once Seaman

had been released by Arsenal. However, his stay at City was short lived as a back injury forced the former England number one to retire after just 26 appearances in all competitions.

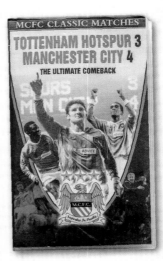

deadly form of meningitis.

I'd barely left his side for two weeks but had a ticket for the game. Friends offered lifts, but I couldn't leave his side. Instead, I watched the Spurs goals flooding in on my Nokia 6410, and remember thinking to myself, "Thanks City, you couldn't even give me a result to lift my mood."

So what followed was simply fantastic, and it gave me a massive boost. Harvey, now 18, also went on to stage his very own remarkable comeback as he made an almost full recovery. Despite amputations to his hands and feet, he's the bubbly little character by my side on matchdays.

At the time it felt like the 4-3 result was sent from above to cheer us up. Typical City!

Keeper Árni Arason's match shirt from the 2003/04 FA Cup fourth-round tie against Spurs – one of the greatest Cup comebacks of modern times.

This fixture has such a special meaning to me as my lad Harvey-James was in a nearby London hospital, just nine months old and fighting for his life against meningococcal septicaemia, a

TREVOR
SINCLAIR

Boyhood City fan Trevor Sinclair arrived at Maine Road in a £3.3 million deal from West Ham, following their relegation from the Premier League. It wasn't long before he had cemented his place in club history by scoring the first ever competitive goal for City at the COMS, in a UEFA Cup win over Welsh side TNS.

This classy, self-striped home shirt was the first of three to be designed and manufacured by Reebok, who had taken over the onerous contract from Le Coq Sportif in time for the 2003/04 Premier League season.

Having notched the first goal at the new stadium, Sinclair followed up his record by chalking up City's first strike at the COMS in a Manchester derby. On January 14th 2006, he opened the scoring in a 3-1 City win.

Sinclair departed City for Cardiff at the end of the 2006/07 season, having scored six goals in a total of 98 appearances.

Preston for £5 million in the final months of Kevin Keegan's 2001/02 promotion campaign. He went on to score some memorable goals, including the winner in the 2004 FA Cup comeback victory at Spurs and one in the first League derby at the COMS, a 4-1 win.

Jon must have realised his City days were numbered when Stuart Pearce put keeper David James up front in his place as City chased a winner and a European spot on the final day of 2004/05.

Jon Macken appeared only twice in this long-sleeved version of Reebok's broad-striped nod to the '60s away shirt, scoring in cup games away to QPR and Leicester.

A former United Youth-team striker, Macken joined from

A landmark jersey in the history of Manchester City, in that it was the last home shirt to be used by the first team for a period of more than one season. The Reebok design boasted a lifespan of two years, 2004-06.

Joey Barton, a product of Jim Cassell's successful Maine Road youth academy, made his City debut away to Bolton Wanderers on 5th April 2003. He played over 140 games before moving on to Newcastle in the summer of 2007.

Paul Bosvelt 2004/05 Premier League

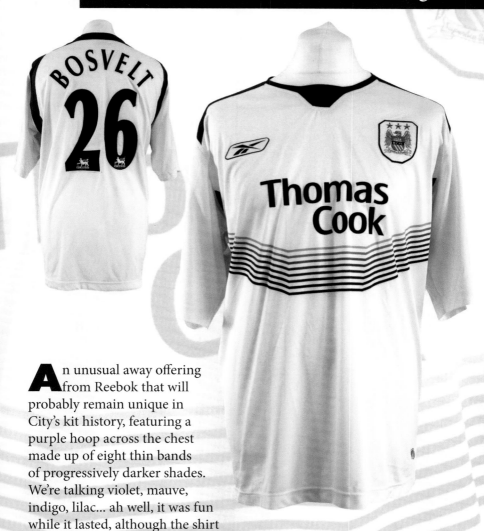

An unusual away offering from Reebok that will probably remain unique in City's kit history, featuring a purple hoop across the chest made up of eight thin bands of progressively darker shades. We're talking violet, mauve, indigo, lilac... ah well, it was fun while it lasted, although the shirt was only pressed into use six times in the 2004/05 season.

Paul Bosvelt, the tough-tackling Dutchman, joined City from Feyenoord at the age of 33, becoming Kevin Keegan's fourth summer signing of 2003, when he joined new boys David Seaman, Michael Tarnet and Trevor Sinclair at the club.

Antoine Sibierski   2004/05 Premier League

First used by City for the 2003/04 campaign, the broad-striped red and black style returned in 2004/05 and was worn three times in the Premier League. The only change was to the sponsor, Thomas Cook having taken over the role after First Advice was declared bankrupt.

The shirt was never available to buy as a replica with the Thomas Cook logo, making it a real collector's item.

French midfielder Antoine Sibierski donned this shirt for games at Everton and West Brom.

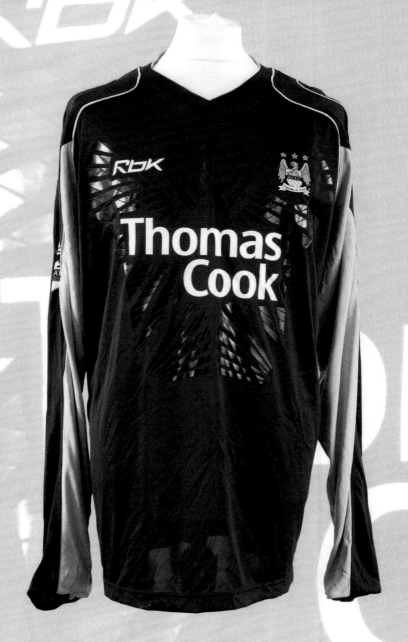

Joe Hart made his City debut wearing this then-futuristic style against Sheffield United on 14th October 2006. Through the season, he competed with Nicky Weaver, Kasper Schmeichel and Andreas Isaksson for the number one slot under Stuart Pearce.

Manufacturers Reebok changed the logo on this season's new shirts, rejecting their geometric pattern for an abbreviated 'Rbk'.

A black asymmetric lower panel with matching shoulder flashes made this yellow Reebok design unique in City kit history – which is to say we've never seen anything like it since.

Full of promise, Irish midfielder Stephen Ireland upgraded to his more favoured number seven shirt for the following 2006/07 campaign, having established himself in the first team.

The 2006/07 Premier League match shirt which marked Reebok's final season as designer and manufacturer.

Buzzing Scots striker Paul Dickov ranks high among City fans' true cult heroes, and he will always be mentioned with reverence for that incredible last-minute equaliser at Wembley back in 1999. Paul still sparkles in his role as club ambassador on matchdays.

Michael Ball wore this admirably plain shirt through the whole 90 minutes of City's 2-1 Premier League victory at Old Trafford on 10th February 2008, which coincided with the 50th anniversary of the 1958 Munich air disaster.

City's shirt sponsors, together with the new manufacturer, agreed to have their branding removed from the kit on this one occasion.

The selfless decision by Thomas Cook.com and Le Coq Sportif came after talks were held between the companies and supporters' groups, the outcome of which included various initiatives and a kit that incorporated a black ribbon of remembrance.

On the field of play, City grabbed our first victory at Old Trafford since 1973/74, when that Denis Law backheel relegated United And, on the shirt, the centrally positioned badge also signalled the return of a mid-'70s style.

After five years of Reebok designing and producing the City shirt, the club returned to Le Coq Sportif for the seasons 2007/08 and 2008/09.

One of the attractive qualities of the shirts of this era was the manufacturer's modest willingness to set their logo on top of the shoulder, leaving the front beautifully uncluttered. Hats off to them for the purple and white striped away shirt, this one issued to defender Nedum Onuoha.

Signed by Sven Goran-Eriksson from Atlético Madrid during the summer of 2007, Bulgarian winger Petrov spent three seasons with City before moving on to Bolton Wanderers. His cult-figure status among Blues supporters was enhanced yet further when he returned to Manchester in 2013 to play a full 90 minutes for amateur side Chorlton Torpedo, scoring the only goal of the game as they beat Spartak Brushes 1-0.

Le Coq Sportif's adventurous design for this 2007/08 third shirt ran to an asymmetric shoulder panel, which always seemed an odd position for the City badge.

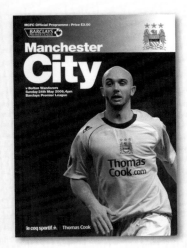

Another Premier League home shirt by Le Coq Sportif that appears relatively 'classic' in design, agreeably plain at first glance, only to reveal subtle contemporary tweaks on further inspection – namely, those asymmetrical shoulder panels and insets on one flank and the inner sleeves.

Brazilian Berti managed to be named on City's bench 20 consecutive times in his solitary season at the club before being given his ten minutes of fame on the last game of the season at home to Bolton, earning himself real cult status along the way.

Michael Johnson 2008/09 UEFA Cup

This groundbreaking orange shirt was issued to Michael Johnson for the 2008/09 UEFA Cup campaign, which saw City bow out at the quarter-final stage to Hamburg.

Designed by Le Coq Sportif, flying in the face of tradition in their final season before City returned to Umbro, the shirt features plastic name and number sets under UEFA rules, where they were made of felt for the Premier League shirts.

Shaun Wright-Phillips' match-worn shirt from the pre-season friendly match against Scottish giants Celtic on 8th August 2009.

The admirably restrained, round-collared shirt was the first designed by Umbro since 1997.

This shirt was kindly donated to the collection by former Blues player Willo Flood, who swapped after the Celtic game which City won 2-1. Years earlier, Flood had progressed together with SWP through City's academy.

Vincent Kompany's matchworn shirt from the Premier League home fixture against Tottenham on 5th May 2010 – which I'm curiously proud to reveal is unwashed. That fact alone brings the springtime evening, the Etihad atmosphere, the legendary player himself that much closer. Shame City lost the match 1-0!

Kompany used the number 33 for two seasons before switching to number 4 at the start of 2010/11. Signed from Hamburg in 2008 aged just 22, the Belgian initially operated in midfield before going on to establish himself as one of the world's finest centre-halves. Eleven seasons with City, eleven major trophies. And currently the last City player to be awarded a testimonial, which he used to help raise funds for Manchester's homeless.

The dual-coloured sash style is one of the most popular used for City away shirts, first adopted back in the 1972/73 season.

Not a lot of people know that City actually used three away shirts in that one campaign: the white sash style which was echoed here; a dark blue shirt with a red and white sash which was introduced for away games where the white clashed with the home team; and, finally, a black and red striped jersey was worn away in the League at Coventry. It was 30 years before City used the sash style again, in 2002/03, when Le Coq Sportif gave it a welcome revival.

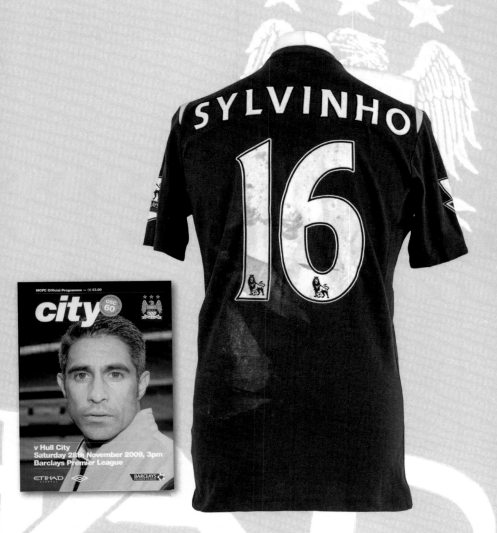

Brazilian left-back Sylvinho wore Umbro's grey, 'jeans-friendly' third shirt at Burnley on 3rd April 2010, when City recorded an emphatic 6-1 win.

Replaced by Nigel De Jong in the 67th minute following an injury,

Sylvinho generously paused and gifted his shirt to City fan Mark Gilligan as he was helped in the direction of the dugouts.

And why is this a unique City shirt? It's the only one ever to feature epaulettes!

Featuring unique felt FA Cup and FA Respect sleeve logos and an unmistakably authentic, still-fragrant Vick stain for additional provenance, here is Mario Balotelli's shirt worn during the first half of City's 2011 FA Cup semi-final at Wembley.

It proved a typically eventful afternoon for City's maverick Italian striker, as United's Rio Ferdinand didn't take kindly to the cheeky wink aimed at him after the final whistle. But by then Yaya Touré's first-half strike had settled the match, and now many of the Blues faithful were starting to believe the tide was turning finally in Manchester football.

Touré would again prove to be the main man with the winner in the ensuing final victory over Stoke City, ensuring City sealed their first piece of major silverware for 35 years.

Micah Richards' matchworn Premier League shirt from City's historic and unforgettable 2011/12 season.

The former Youth team skipper appeared 29 times as City clinched their first top-flight title for 44 years. Playing at right-back, he also contributed a goal and no less than five assists across all competitions.

Umbro's retro red and black-striped away shirt ticked all the boxes for the City traditionalists, except perhaps for the black sleeves which gave the (deliberate?) impression that an undershirt was being worn.

The original, inspirational striped away shirt was the brainchild of maverick assistant boss Malcolm Allison, who sought to emulate the style and success of AC Milan. As it turned out, the experiment was a roaring success as City wore the change strip against Leicester when they lifted the 1969 FA Cup,

then again in the ensuing 1970 ECWC final victory in Vienna against Gornik Zabrze, and yet again, just nine days later, in their League Cup win over West Brom.

This is dependable stopper Joleon Lescott's long-sleeved shirt from City's 2-2 draw away at Fulham on 18th September 2011.

The now-iconic 'Aguero moment' shirt from 2011/12 will be forever remembered for City's first top-flight title win in living memory. The waves woven into the texture of the shirt represented the sound waves made by the City crowd singing 'Blue Moon', while the texturing recalls the perforated Aertex style once worn in warm weather back in the day.

This shirt was worn by Carlos Tevez in a 3-0 win over Wigan Athletic on 10th September 2011, and was sourced direct from a former club employee who was gifted the shirt. It was a controversial season for the Argentine striker who infamously went on strike between September and March after a falling out with boss Roberto Mancini during a Champions' League group stage match at Bayern Munich.

ssued to Edin Džeko during the 2012/13 season, this Umbro home shirt saw a fleeting return to the 'phantom undershirt' look prevalent in the '90s.

It would be the last campaign where Umbro produced the City shirt, ending a relationship that went back to the 1934 FA Cup final when they designed and made the kit for both City and Portsmouth. Rumour had it that the kit made such an impression on manager Wilf Wild that he personally wrote to Umbro, explaining how delighted and impressed the team were with the shirts.

Signed by Roberto Mancini from Wolfsburg in January 2011, Džeko often divided opinion among City fans. Many regard his finest hour as the time he hit four in City's 5-1 victory at Tottenham in August 2011, while his equalising goal from the bench in City's iconic final-day win over QPR in 2011/12 is often overlooked.

Following his arrival from Shakhtar Donetsk in the summer of 2014, 'Dino' went on to become one of the most respected City midfielders of the modern era.

He wore Nike's debut home shirt on 11th May 2014 in the 2-0 home win against West Ham United – the title-clinching fixture, on the last day of the season, which meant the brilliant Brazilian had picked up both Premier League and League Cup winner's medals in his first season in English football.

An instant touch of class from Nike: a classic round collar and asymmetric dual stripes in their first season as City kit manufacturers. Meanwhile, on the back of the shirt, an unusual typewriter-style font was used in City's Champions' League fixtures.

Spanish striker Álvaro Negredo wore this short for the 2013/14 CL match against CSKA Moscow on 23rd October.

152

Another mixture of tradition and modern experimentation from the designers at Nike.

Then the regular England number one, Joe Hart generously launched his yellow (and faded lime green) shirt into the away end after the game at Chelsea on 31st January 2015. It was caught by City fan Ryan Leicester, adding fantastic provenance to the shirt he later donated into the collection.

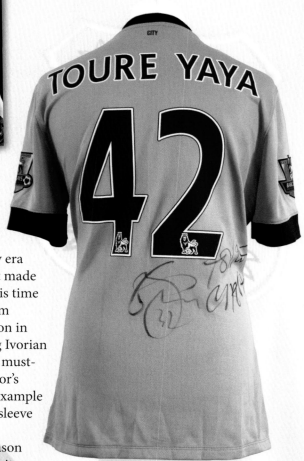

Few players from any era can rival the impact made by Yaya Touré during his time at City after joining from Barcelona for £24 million in 2010. The commanding Ivorian midfielder's shirts are a must-have in any City collector's collection, this signed example with navy trim and PL sleeve patches dating back to 2014/15, the second season Nike supplied the City kits.

After showing his former boss Pep Guardiola the way from the Camp Nou to the Etihad, Touré went on to appear 292 times overall for City, scoring no less than 81 goals, including timely big-match FA Cup semi-final and final-winning strikes.

Yaya's farewell appearance came during the Blues' Centurion season against Brighton & Hove Albion on 9th May 2018.

Local centre-back Tosin Adara-bioyo's first-team chances were strictly limited to cup games, but he made his full City debut in the FA Cup fifth-round match at Chelsea on 21st February 2016.

This was after Manuel Pellegrini opted to play a weakened side five days before travelling to play Real Madrid in the Champions' League semi-final second leg.

In true City style, we had crashed out of both competitions before the week was out.

After a 19-year absence, Nike's new City home shirt for 2016/17 saw a return to the traditional round club badge, much to the delight of many Blues.

When Raheem Sterling joined City on a five-year deal for an initial sum of £44 million, he became the most expensive English player at that time. Over six years, his goal ratio of one in every three City games is making the regular England international look like a real bargain.

Sterling's shirt from the 3-0 Premier League victory at Hull City on Boxing Day 2016 was given to the Tigers' Welsh international centre-back James Chester after the match.

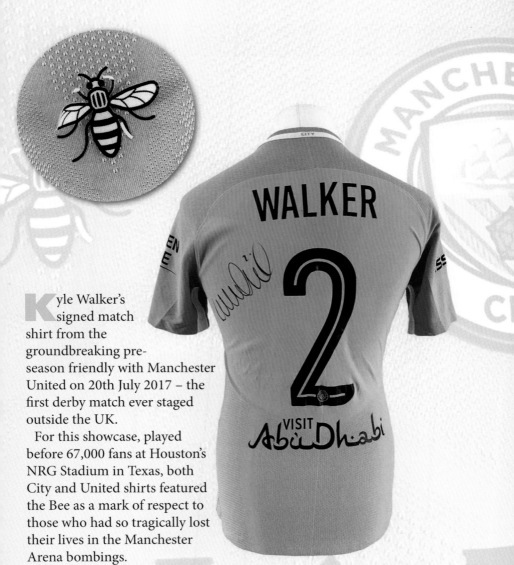

Kyle Walker's signed match shirt from the groundbreaking pre-season friendly with Manchester United on 20th July 2017 – the first derby match ever staged outside the UK.

For this showcase, played before 67,000 fans at Houston's NRG Stadium in Texas, both City and United shirts featured the Bee as a mark of respect to those who had so tragically lost their lives in the Manchester Arena bombings.

Come the start of the season proper, the big-money signing from Spurs would suffer an ignominious home debut, sent off against Everton. But the full-back's class was seen to prevail over the course of the season, as City lifted both the League Cup and the Premier League trophy in the first ever Centurion season. Personally, Walker experienced defeat in just one of his 32 League games played.

The Poppy symbol was first introduced to City shirts at the Remembrance Day fixture in the 2003/04 season – when curiously not all of the players' jerseys included the addition.

Poppy shirts have since become sought-after items for collectors, not only representing an extra variation to a shirt each season, but also a universally popular and deserving charity cause.

This customised 2017/18 away shirt was worn by Kevin De Bruyne at West Brom (a 3-2 away win) on 28th October 2017, and was gifted to a fan as the team departed the Hawthorns.

John Stones' signed shirt from the end-of-season fixture at Southampton on 13th May 2018 – a match that saw history made.

With City needing three points to become the first ever 100-point champions, Gabriel Jesus scored with virtually the the last kick of an outstanding campaign to secure a 1-0 victory and a record-breaking three-figure tally. The City side were Centurions!

This shirt belongs to my lad Harvey, who was thrilled to receive it as a gift from City's French-born, Spanish international stopper Aymeric Laporte after the 2-1 Champions' League victory over Hoffenheim, an unforgettable occasion as guests of the club which I referred to earlier.

The Nike home shirt is in the retro 'grandad' style, featuring a single button with no collar.

On the night, an unstoppable Leroy Sané hit both goals to ensure the Blues secured top spot and group qualification.

Unfortunately, City would then go on to fall at the quarter-final stage of the competition following an exciting second-leg fixture against Tottenham – although, the less about that one the better.

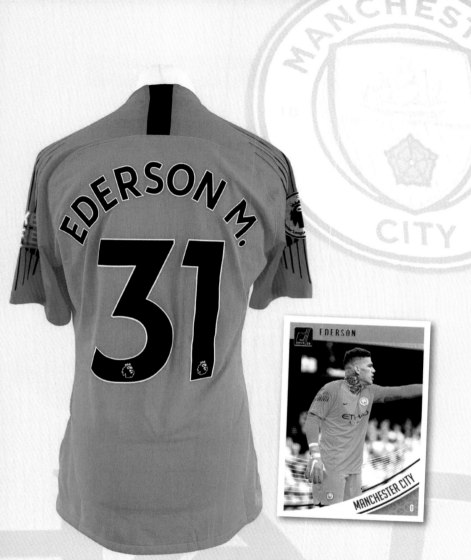

The two-time Golden Glove winner joined City from Benfica in the summer of 2017, in time to enjoy a trophy-laden spell at the club. This shirt was worn on Wednesday 6th February 2019 away to Everton in a 2-0 Blues win which would become part of City's historic domestic Treble season.

The brilliant Brazilian, who "only cost £30 million," (as the song goes) is known for his amazing distribution and calmness on the ball, with many Blues claiming he would be equally well suited in a central midfield role.

Here is David Silva's signed shirt from the Premier League match against West Ham United on 24th November 2018. Silva didn't only captain the side that Saturday but also scored the opening goal in a 4-1 victory – and, of course, any fanatical, compulsive collector will recognise how much of that magic remains encapsulated in the shirt itself. It was donated by David himself in aid of the hugely worthy Isla Caton fundraising appeal.

The shirt worn by Gündoğan during City's epic FA Cup quarter-final comeback against Swansea City, when the Blues came back from trailing 2-0 at half-time to win 3-2.

Elated by the result, the German midfielder threw the shirt into the away end after the final whistle. It was only a few weeks later that I was contacted via social media by the very City supporter who had caught it, asking if I was interested in adding the shirt to my collection. The answer is almost always a resounding 'yes'.

For 2019's 125th Anniversary Community Shield match, outfield players wore a shirt with a one-off, minimal, traditional design while the keepers received a shirt that was yet more low key, based on a standard teamwear template from Puma with ironed-on name and numbers.

Mahrez was originally selected but City officials were concerned with a tablet he had been given while on international duty with Algeria, so insisted he be checked as a precaution. Leroy Sané replaced him and, in typical City style, was injured in the first ten minutes, ultimately having to wait a year to complete his transfer from Bayern Munich. Meanwhile, Mahrez's test came back completely clear, meaning he could have started. At least we beat Liverpool in the penalty shoot-out.

Arguably one of City's greatest players of the modern era, David Silva just oozed class from the moment he arrived at City from Valencia during the summer of 2010. What followed was ten years of fantastic service and week-in, week-out top performances.

Elegant on the ball, with superb vision, Silva contributed to everything good that happened during his long spell at the club, which saw him pick up four Premier League titles, two FA Cups and four League Cups.

Nicknamed 'The Magician' by his adoring City followers, Silva quietly went about his business as the ultimate professional, always managing to maintain a low profile outside of the game.

As with the great Colin Bell, Silva will always be remembered and spoken of in high regard, as befitting a player with a statue in his honour at the Etihad.

Aymeric Laporte's personally signed shirt, worn by the centre-back in the home match against Arsenal on June 17th 2020, a comfortable 3-0 win.

The occasion was City's first game back following the suspension of football due to the Covid-19 pandemic – what would prove to be the only game where this exact style was used.

Later shirts would also be emblazoned with a 'Black Lives Matter' sleeve patch and lettering in place of the player's name on the reverse, as well as an NHS patch and 'Citizens Giving' panel on the front. The element that makes this design a one-off, and a real collector's item in turn, is the BLM patch which changed to all black after this initial fixture.

Number 100 in our journey through 101 matchworn City shirts is, fittingly, this spare, unnumbered jersey from the 100th FA Cup final between City and Spurs. It recalls a match that we all know was decided by a replay. We also know that Steve McKenzie scored the greatest FA Cup goal of the 1980s in the return match at Wembley, which was nevertheless widely overlooked by many due to the outcome.

Umbro only produced the one set of shirts for the final, which was used for both games, while opponents Spurs used two sets. The players were given a long- and short-sleeve shirt option for the final, where only Dave Bennett plumped for the long sleeves. In the replay, both he and Nicky Reid chose to go 'long'.

Now the hunt is on to find a numbered shirt that actually played a part in the match, though it's impossible to widen my search any further. This shirt was donated by fellow collector and Blue, Will Kerfoot, all the way from Australia.

Puma's 2020/21 Champions' League shirt may resemble a sheet of cracked ice, but City skated past Marseille with a 3-0 win in the group match on 9th December 2020.

Phil Foden, 'the Stockport Iniesta', enjoyed a fantastic CL campaign in which City reached our first ever final. Displaying an immense natural talent, the die-hard Blue quickly rose through the academy ranks to become a key member of Pep Guardiola's first-team squad. An England international and double Premier League title winner by the age of 21 – and a potential future City captain.

Author

Mark McCarthy's amazing City journey began aged just eight following a visit to his grandfather's house one Sunday afternoon in December 1983, when he was told that his cousin Mick had just signed for the Blues. An obsessive City fan from that moment on, Mark would dream of owning a shirt from Mick's time at the club. Once that dream was achieved, years later, it kicked off a fixation on collecting matchworn City shirts. His total now stands at 410... and counting.

Acknowledgements

To write a book has always been a dream for me, so to write one on a subject I'm so passionate about makes it twice as special; but without the fantastic support and encouragement of my lovely wife, Sarah McCarthy, it may never have got off the ground. Thank you, Sarah, and also to my children Lucie, Jordan, Harvey and Olivia for always remaining interested when I was relaying yet another shirt tale. This also applies to my work colleague Nigel Hughes who has no interest in shirts or football but whose enthusiasm to remain interested holds no boundaries. Thanks to Stephanie Alexander-Jinks for all her help at the start, to Paul and Jane Bloomfield for their constant encouragement, to Gary and Derek at Conker Editions who have been so easy to work with, and to photographer Caroline Brown. Imagewise, thanks to Josh Langton for p181, to David Morcom Photography for p117 and to WellOffside.com for the book's Brother endpapers. Many thanks to everyone who has helped me secure a shirt or pointed me in the right direction over the years. Finally, a special mention to my father-in-law Brian Alexander for all his hard work in restoring badly framed shirts, his ability and patience are second to none.

Wanted

Do you have a City matchworn shirt hidden away or stored in the loft? Did you catch a City shirt thrown into the crowd, have a relative who played for the club or win a shirt in a raffle? I'm always looking to add to the collection.

Contact me via the following:
Email: mmmac@hotmail.co.uk
Facebook: Manchester City Match Worn Shirts **Twitter:** @MarkMmmac
Instagram: @manchester_city_match_shirts_

Teamwork...

Sarah McCarthy | Kevin Mulvaney | Johnny Doak | Steven Holmes
Robert Taylor | Gavin Woodrow | Stirling Sievey | Billy Pointer
Lee Taylor | Les Motherby | Michael Cookson | Andrew Shaw
Greg Braniff | Nigel Gregory | Phil Batty | Anya Macdonald | Rob Kerr
Graeme Fussell | Andrew Wilson | Tina Clews | Phil Clews
Jason Dugdale | Asa @FootballCreatio | Graham Lamb | Dave Coop
Alfie Lancaster | Gary Kearney | Samara Henry-Riding
Steve Robinson | Dan Robinson | Mark Beetson | Ian O'Connor
Steven Gardner | Harvey-James McCarthy | Liv Judd | Eric Low
David Meikleham | Peter McNally | Tal, Liam & Daniel McNally
Davy Byrne | Iain Cameron | Jane Judd | Gary Sullivan | Tom Bunting
Christopher Ballagher | Andrew Appleby | Paul Fineran | Chris Keane
Rodney George | Graham Bowie | John Harris | Robert Carney
Mark Bonello | John Spellman | Neil Spellman | David Warner
Grzegorz Szczech - Polish Blues | Paul Whelan | Andrew Schilling
Pete Schilling | Jon Swanton | Andrew Jepson | Nigel Rothband
Andrew Tanner | Andrew Lakie | Rachel Doyle | Josh Shaw
Stephen Carter | Jason Blue King | Mark & Rudi Lewis
Louise Powis | Samuel Brightwell | Ian Gregory
Nicola Wilson | Graeme Waite | Simon Hynes
Gordon Hyslop | Chris & Terry Hall
Alistair Hay | Phillip Gatenby | Joe Stanaway
David Leach | Thomas Herskind Olesen
Nick Fish | Marcus Bayley | Neville Bayley
Stephen (Harry the B) Harrison
Alan Heffernan | Terry Mallon
David Sacks | Kevin Hughes | Mike Hughes
Martin McNelis | Steven Morton

185

Tinarom Yamprasert | Matthew Donovan | John McNaught

Henry Proudlock | William & Tom Trimble | Carol Johnson

Gary James | James Doyle | Charlie Tiger Smith | James Wilkinson

Alun Jones | Richard McDonald | Phil Wilson | Andy Parkin

Justin Handby | Russell Osborne | Oliver Otto | Gavin Haigh

Brian Houghton @CityonaCard | Marc James Hince

John Leigh | David Ramsay | Gary Stanford | Owain Clarke

Bernard Wood | Keith Lumb | Graham Keogh | Vincent Waldron

The Needle Wizard | Richard Anscombe | Marco Mozzachiodi

David Crook | Andy Turner - Man City Fan TV | Nicholas Price

Stuart Anderson | Peris Hatton | Jim Hawkins | Calum Johnson

Paul Cadwallader | Darren Farghaly | David Butler | Mick Coogan

Matthew McCutcheon @Kilmarnock Matchworn Shirts | Cian Bebb

Claire, Harry & Oliver | Philip Banerjee | Alexander Savidge

Aleksandar Savić | Charlie Wharam | Roger Reade | Jo Couchman

Rob, Dan & Nick Ball | Russell Askew | Lorraine Murray | Matt Lee

Neville Evans | Joseph Carroll | Steve Spurgeon | Mike Buckley

Liam Ogden & Bill Ogden | Tim Selby | Paul Southwood

Dave & Harrison Bennett | Jamie Fox | Paul Hughes

Alan Arenson | Dermot Lucking | Antony Smith

Chris Little | Robert Knott | Jeremy Griffiths

Tim Anstee | Ben Clarke | John Bishop

Phil Moody | Mark Gilligan | Nick Gee

Ian Douglas | Chris Jinks | Peter Burt

Chris Worrall | Gary Price | Ian Felce

Claire Gardiner | Carl Richmond

Heather, Karen & John Battison

Caroline Banks | David G Hall

Graham A Hall | Noel O'Brien

Darren Clarke | Mark Roberts

Martin Travers | Pete Doyle

Simon Haselden | Gill Scully

Bessie Scully | Alan Parke | Stephanie Alder | Murray Alexander
Rob Kerr | Thomas Kerr | Grant Young | Rick Wilcock | Sam Wilcock
Paul Diggett | Kenneth Boyle | Andrew Cleaver | Cían Walker
Ian Stoney | Andrew Brookfield | Paul Clifford | Ian Lees | Chi Tsui
Stephen Askew | Charlotte Askew | Jack Carruthers | Leo Carruthers
Alan Blamires | Gary Pelham | Helen Clarke | Thomas O'Dowd
Dan Jobber | Grant Spink | Darren Banks | John Devlin | John P
Stephen Mee | Steven Titterton | Matthew Higgins | Ian Olver
Philip, Archie & Leni Barber | Geoff Cornish | Lindsay Marriott
Maureen Sadler | Derek Richmond | Ben Curley | Stuart Williamson
Wayne Smith | Alistair Brookhouse | Harold & Christine English
Steve Plant - Wolves Matchworn | Phil Burrows | Scott Game
Tiernan Jinks | Oscar Wayne | Andrew Waldon | Neil Shaw | Jim Ferris
Peter Gregory | Neil Mather | Barton Geoffrey Pelham | Ian Davies
Lorenz Schumacher - www.fcbtrikots.ch | Caroline Brown
Andrew Sheldon | Darren Reid | James Marshall | Phil Holmes
Tony Munro | Lauren Knott | Susan Bookbinder | David Sheel
Stuart Milne | Ed Felton | Daniel Shaw | Jason Clarkson | Jack Banner
Damian Worden | Adrian Sherratt | Oakley Kelly
John Roughton | Joshua Langton | Anthony Smith
Brandon Thompson | Bartley Ramsay | William Bell
Colin Lindley | Steven Wilson | Karen Seas
Bramwell Jinks | Jordan-Lee McCarthy
Emma Dawn Hammett | Neale A Burns
David Griffiths | Mohd Fakhri Sooti
Mark Burns | Martin Shaw | John Spellman
Adrian Webster | David Golden
Greig Morrison | Steve Bootle
Guy Whitfield | Bluebell Jinks
Steve Slack | Laurence Myers
Lexi Burns | Tiah Burns | Karl Evans
Howard McCarthy

101
MANCHESTER
CITY
MATCHWORN
SHIRTS

**The Players - The Matches
The Stories Behind the Shirts**

101
MANCHESTER
CITY
MATCHWORN
SHIRTS

**The Players - The Matches
The Stories Behind the Shirts**

MAIDEN

1237

umbro

bro